THE ART OF GOLF

1754-1940

THE $\mathcal{A}$RT OF GOLF

1754-1940

*Timeless, enchanting illustrations and narrative
of golf's formative years*

GARY H. SCHWARTZ

MAGAZINE COVERS AND ILLUSTRATIONS
PICTURE POSTCARDS
ADVERTISING ILLUSTRATIONS

WOOD RIVER PUBLISHING
TIBURON, CALIFORNIA

The Art of Golf
1754–1940

© 1990

by

Gary H. Schwartz

Wood River Publishing
680 Hawthorne Drive
Tiburon, CA 94920

First Edition April 1990

Design: Gabrielle Disario
Editing: Lee Berman
Copy Photography: Martin Zeitman
Printing: Toppan Printing Co. Singapore

Library of Congress Cataloging in Publication Data

Schwartz, Gary H., 1949–

The Art of Golf 1754–1940:
Timeless, enchanting illustrations and narrative of
golf's formative years
p.   cm.
ISBN: 0-9623000-1-0

1. Golf in art.   2. Drawing.   I. Title
NC825. G64S39 1990
741.6-dc20   89-28182

TABLE OF CONTENTS

Cover photo of golf course courtesy of Mauna Kea Beach Hotel.
Title page illustration: The Queen, The Lady's Newspaper. *1907.*

INTRODUCTION

"Such uninterrupted exercise, cooperating with the keen air from the sea, must, without all doubt, keep the appetite on edge, and steel the constitution against all the common attacks of distemper."

Early description of golf
by Tobias Smollett, 1771

Artists, illustrators and photographers of the past have left behind a wonderful visual world of graphic material depicting the evolution of golf. What better way to appreciate the rise of golf to its eminent position in worldwide sports than by looking at the vehicles that originally represented the sport to the public: the magazine, the picture postcard, and popular advertising.

This volume begins in the mid-eighteenth century, with the opening of the renowned St. Andrews Golf Club in Scotland. The selections of art reproduced in the plates portray the infancy and growth of both golf and graphic illustration in the United States and the world. The result is a visual record of human ideas and social movements, as well as significant historical moments in the evolution of golf as a sport. These works vividly highlight social, cultural and commercial fads and trends from the time of St. Andrews in 1754 to the onset of World War II in 1940, which marked the end of golf's formative years. Of further interest is the surprising discovery that magazine covers, postcards and even advertisements during this period were designed with such imagination and beauty.

Prior to the 1880s, when golf began its period of dramatic growth in Great Britain and the United States, few working class people had the time or resources for outdoor amusement. Other sports, such as cricket, lawn tennis, archery and polo were introduced in the United States before 1875, but were slow to gain a following. An additional reason for the slow acceptance of these sports was an American suspicion of any games imported from Britain.

Yet another factor affected golf's slow initial acceptance. The general public in the United States and many of the nations of the world were primarily sports spectators, not participants. Horse racing and prizefighting were constantly in the papers; baseball in the United States was on the rise. One exception was the rising popularity of cycling, but only for men. Most women in skirts could not expect to comfortably mount the high-wheel bicycle.

The fact was that up until the 1880s no one popular activity had really emerged as a vehicle for mass recreation. That all changed with a dramatic rise in interest in golf in the United States and much of the world, that marked the decade of the 1880s. At the same time, popular exposure of the sport in magazines, advertising and picture postcards finally showed the world what fun it could be to knock a ball around.

In the early 1800s the sport of golf and the art of graphic illustration were highly specialized and not yet generally accessible to the public worldwide. As the cost of reproducing illustrations decreased, however, more and more magazine, postcard and advertising art relating to golf was offered to the growing middle class. Thus the growth of the sport paralleled its increasing popularity in the visual media.

New worlds were opened to people who discovered golf through printed images. Each visual resource played an important part in the public's perception of golf and helped pique their interest. The sport began a growth spurt from a modest few thousand players that has culminated in the tens of millions who avidly participate today.

Golf's formative years culminated in 1940, with the second World War. With the onset of war, international competition was suspended. At the same time, key technological advances in equipment began to appear. Coinciding with these developments were changes in the popular coverage of golf through magazine illustrations, advertisements and picture postcards. Increasingly photo-journalism was to replace the work of magazine, advertising and postcard illustrators.

The post-World War II era marks the emergence of golf as a big business. This growing commercial success has made golf more accessible to the public than ever before. With more courses, better equipment and improved techniques more players daily are turning this sport of aristocrats into the sport of millions.

The graphic works in this compilation show the cultural, social and commercial roles of the sport from 1754 to 1940, including changes in clothing, equipment, technique, course development, and public perceptions.

Many of the pictures in this volume depict golf in an insightful, sensitive manner at a time when it was largely an elite, amateur pastime. The public tended to associate golf with romance, leisure and fashion. Men and women alike had to be properly dressed for the occasion. For early women golfers this involved an impractical cotton dress; for men, fanciful tweeds and a fine tie.

Some of the graphics include touches of romance and sensuality. We encounter an idealized woman holding golf clubs, as though she was on the links nearly every day, with perfect hair, wearing a glorious dress and, of course, a fashionable sun hat.

Viewing these illustrations also shows us that the same adventurous spirit that inspired the early golf pioneers still characterizes the golfer of today. The thrill and exhilaration of people participating in the sport of golf certainly has not changed, although the style of their visual portrayal has evolved considerably.

Imagine now what it would be like to be among the first pioneers to carve out a rough course in a pasture and drive a *feathery* towards a distant hole. See yourself in front of a jazzy new automobile at a world class golf resort. Feel the sun, the challenge, and the excitement as you tee off on a new adventure in sport...and in art. ❧

"Hard by, in the fields called the Links, the citizens of Edinburgh divert themselves at a game called Golf, in which they use a curious kind of bats tipped with horn, and small elastic balls of leather, stuffed with feathers, rather less than tennis balls, but of a much harder consistence. These they strike with such force and dexterity from one hole to another, that they will fly to an incredible distance. Of this diversion the Scots are so fond, that, when the weather will permit, you may see a multitude of all ranks, from the senator of justice to the lowest tradesman, mingled together, in their shirts, and following the balls with the utmost eagerness."

—Tobias Smollett, 1771

An early Dutch form of golf, from the sixteenth century.

A fashionable kolf *court in eighteenth-century Amsterdam.*

Of all of mankind's inventions, the one that has given the greatest pleasure has been the ball. It is so wonderfully versatile that it is unsurpassed in the endless hours of enjoyment it brings to old and young alike.

Physically the ball can de dealt with in four ways. It can be thrown, caught, kicked and hit. It can also be produced in different sizes and shapes. Over time, a multitude of games have evolved from various different types of balls. The evolution of these games is not always clearly documented. This uncertainty regarding origins applies equally to the game of golf and the people who gave it to the world.

It is commonly believed that the Scots invented the game, although there is a school of thought, and indeed some evidence, that the Dutch were the first to begin swatting a ball with some sort of club. A sport called colf or kolf was played in and around Holland centuries ago. The Dutch claim is bolstered by several paintings, done in the late sixteenth and early seventeenth centuries, showing small children holding implements that are unmistakably the size and shape of golf clubs. However, players used these clubs primarily in indoor settings, often in a small, covered, courtyard. Although the game may have been a forerunner of golf, it more nearly resembled croquet or hockey.

According to legend, golf began in Scotland when a shepherd, whiling away the time, whacked a small stone with his stick and saw the stone fall, to his astonishment, into a rabbit hole. Quite naturally, he tried to duplicate the feat, and doubtless became the first man ever

A variation of golf as played in France in 1497.

Child of seventeenth-century Holland.

A St. Nicholas Party, by Dutch artist Jan Steen, depicting a gift of a kolf *club to a young boy. c. 1670.*

to three-putt. Whatever the actual facts of its origin, the game developed in Scotland, and it was the Scots who subsequently blessed the world with their game.

By the mid-1400s, the Scots enjoyed their primitive game of *golfe* so much that, in 1457, Scotland's Parliament of King James II declared it illegal. Anyone caught playing the game was fined and imprisoned because the King was afraid skill at golf would replace skill with the bow and arrow necessary to the defense of the realm. To James, hitting a bull's-eye was far more important than sinking a golfe shot.

But the game of golf could not be kept from the people. In spite of three separate edicts against playing the sport, noblemen continued to play in pastures by the sea, and the game continued to be a popular amusement.

The proscription against golf in Scotland remained in effect until the introduction of gunpowder near the end of the fifteenth century lessened the importance of archery. Golf was restored as a legal sport to the people in the mid-1500s. Another contributing factor in the legalization of the sport was the fact that royalty took a liking to the game. In 1502, King James IV of Scotland acquired a set of clubs and balls from a bow maker in Australia. In 1567, Mary Queen of Scots was rebuked for playing at Seton House too soon after the death of her husband.

Golf in Scotland remained a sport of the people. There appear to have been no social barriers among participants, royalty and commoners often playing together. Because most golf links in Scotland were publicly owned, and because the northern latitude provided summer daylight from 3 a.m. to 11 p.m., both the working class and the leisure class found opportunities to use them. Thus, golf established an early democratic tradition in Scotland.

Until the structured organization of Golf Clubs emerged in the 1700s, there were no well-defined, well-tended courses on which to play. The earliest Scottish links land was designed entirely by nature. A typical links consisted of high, windswept sand dunes and of hollows where grass grew if the soil was substantial enough. The terrain of a links land usually dictated the route a player would follow. Golfers who batted their *featheries* about a link naturally aimed their shots for the playable grass areas. The dunes were to be avoided. There were no trees or ponds on these ancient links, but there were numerous natural hazards. There were also no greens or wooden tees. The holes were rough-cut, becoming larger and rougher with the passage of time as players took sand from them to make crude tees when driving off. The putting areas exhibited the same bristly grass that grew everywhere else.

The earliest Golf Clubs brought organization, rules and socialization to the game, as well as maintenance of fine golf courses. The first known organized Golf Club was founded in 1744, with the establishment of the Honourable Company of Edinburgh Golfers, which survived until 1831. Ten years later, in 1754, the St. Andrews Society of Golfers came into existence. This organization, now known as the Royal and Ancient Golf Club of St. Andrews, has been in continuous operation since that time.

With the advent of Golf Clubs, standards of play evolved. Many of golf's basic rules of play and competition can be traced to St. Andrews. Until the middle of the eighteenth century, for instance, golf was played over courses of no established length. At the famous Old Course of St. Andrews, golfers *played out* until they reached the *end hole*. There they turned around and *played in* using the same holes. A *round* at St. Andrews came to be eighteen holes. Since St. Andrews soon became the arbiter of all that was correct about golf, eighteen holes was eventually accepted as a standard throughout Scotland and England and subsequently the world.

Early Golf in England

The appealing sport of golf, of course, found its way down from Scotland into England. An early band of Scots first came to England to play golf on a seven-hole course they established at Blackheath, near London, in 1608.

William St. Clair of Roslin, Scotland, who founded the first Golf Club in 1744.

Interest in golf continued in England in the early seventeenth century when King James VI of Scotland ascended the throne as King James I of England and took his courtiers to Blackheath. But the English game did not really begin to take shape until the eighteenth century when the first Clubs and Societies were formed, the members meeting in the local hostelry, electing office-bearers, drawing up rules and putting up prizes. The Honourable Company of Golfers at Blackheath, established in 1766, became the first golf club outside Scotland. In the same year the first recorded competition at Blackheath took place.

The first full-fledged links outside of Scotland was called Westward Ho! It opened in Devon, England in 1864. Eventually, both Blackheath and Westward Ho! members were boarding trains to Liverpool to play at Hoylake, on the new links established by the Royal Liverpool Golf Club. It was not until 1890, however, that the first Englishman won a competition called the British Open. By this time English golf courses, Clubs and facilities had improved and expanded greatly as the sport's popularity steadily increased.

The clubhouse of the Royal and Ancient Golf Club at St. Andrews, Scotland.

The Emergence of Modern Golf

From its earliest primitive beginnings, golf in England soon moved into the sphere of eighteenth century polite society. The early clubs in Great Britain were composed of players known as gentlemen golfers. Such organizations were clearly regarded highly among the upper crust. One reason the game grew so quickly in popularity was undoubtedly that its practitioners—typically men of means—had the influence necessary to gain official recognition. Golf continued to be principally a game associated with the wealthy until recent times. And even today, the wealthy are still largely responsible for the administration of the game and its rules.

In golf's early days, no distinction was made between professionals and amateurs, but by degrees the manufacturers of golf clubs and balls grew in expertise. As their craft became more sophisticated, so did the game itself. Challenge matches were arranged over the major courses in Scotland and England. This period marks the beginning of organized competition and of play primarily by foursomes.

Human nature and love of leisure being what they are, it was inevitable that golfers would soon prefer having someone carry their clubs for them. Thus was born the caddie, the first man to make a living at golf. In that sense, the caddie was the forerunner of the golf-club makers, golf professionals and green-keepers of today. The responsibilities of the first caddies included carrying an armful of loose clubs, clearing the course of curious onlookers, frightening off rabbits and retrieving balls from holes that ultimately became elbow deep.

Despite its far-ranging introduction in Britain, golf was still not truly widely known or played as late as the first half of the nineteenth century. In 1860 the golfing world was still primarily elite, with only about thirty-eight Golf Clubs in existence—thirty-four in Scotland, one in England, two in India and one in France. But starting in the mid-1800s several important events and developments combined to capture the attention of the general public.

The first was of major importance. A number of widely publicized golf matches were undertaken on the finest of the Scottish links, including St. Andrews and Musselburgh. Concurrently, the expanding British railway system made it possible for large crowds to travel to such exhibitions. The more adventuresome spectators eventually tried the links themselves.

Another key development was the invention of the grass mower during the Industrial Revolution. Before that, inland golf was not really possible, for grass grew so long in summer that balls were easily lost and play was only practicable in an ordinary meadow in early spring or late summer.

As golf rose in popularity in the United States, around the turn of the century, many professional golfers from the United Kingdom came to America to lend their technical skills in course construction and teaching. Many remained and formed the nucleus of early U.S. professional competition.

The 1920s and 1930s saw tremendous growth of the sport worldwide. By the on-set of World War II in 1940, the sport had been transformed. Golf was now truly a popular avocation, while technical improvements made it far more sophisticated. At last golf was ready for its entrance into the modern age.

Gentlemen golfers of nineteenth-century Scotland.

Gentlemen golfers of eighteenth-century Scotland.

Caddies at Westward Ho! in 1882.

The American 1950s saw the rise of the Age of Arnold Palmer. Palmer's popularity, President Dwight Eisenhower's association with golf, postwar affluence and television all combined to move golf into the class of big-money professional sports and to attract millions of new followers. Ike loved golf and made no secret about it. His public devotion to the game lent it the last bit of respectability it may have lacked. Golf became accessible to the vast American middle class, and television was ready and eager to give people massive doses of the sport. Golf had become big business.

Equipment and Clothing

The history of golf equipment is an integral part of the history of the sport itself. The development of the golf ball and the golf club are interwoven— as improvements were made in one, they occurred in the other. Golf club design evolved in discernible stages in response to new developments in the ball.

The Golf Ball

The history of golf can be divided into three periods, based on the type of ball employed. The standard missile during the early years of golf was made from a hat-full of boiled feathers stuffed into a small leather pouch that was stitched and then hammered until roughly round. *Featheries*, as these balls were known, required a great deal of tedious and skillful craftsmanship. Most ball makers could only make four to six top-quality featheries a day. Unfortunately, the feathery was vulnerable to environmental conditions; it grew heavier when wet, the stitching was inclined to break, and it was unpredictable when putting.

•The feather ball period of golf came to an end around 1848 with the introduction of the guttapercha ball, made from a resin or gum. The *gutties*, as these balls were called, popularized the game greatly. They were much lower in price, lasted longer, gave improved flight, and ran a great deal truer on the greens. As the balls became older and more worn, the scuffs and grazes actually improved the performance of the gutty. New gutties were therefore deliberately scored on manufacture by hammer and chisel to make them more effective.

The end of the nineteenth century heralded the present rubber-ball period. The rubber-wound ball was composed of a small core of guttapercha wound with elastic thread and then encased in an outer shell of guttapercha. This ball was found to fly another 20-30 yards (18-27 meters) farther than the guttapercha ball.

Golf Clubs

The feathery ball used before the mid-1800s was relatively soft on impact, so the earliest clubs did not have to be particularly strong. The shafts were made of hazel or ash and the heads, much longer and shallower than they are today, were blackthorn, beech, apple or pear.

With the advent of the harder gutty in 1848, there was more wear and tear on clubs. This led to the use of leather inserts in the faces of

President Dwight Eisenhower helped spur golf's postwar boom.

Featheries, gutties *and early rubber-core golf balls.*

Early clubmakers at work in the eighteenth century.

Engraving by W. Dendy Sadler, A Winter Evening.

the clubs. More resilient shafts were also necessary and hickory, from North America, proved to be the answer. The end of the nineteenth century also saw an increase in the use of clubs with iron heads, the forerunners of today's irons. Initially they were simply *trouble* clubs, used for escaping from hazards such as ruts in the ground.

The introduction of the rubber ball by the turn of the twentieth century again led to changes in club design and construction. A much harder wood was needed for the head to withstand the greater impact, and it came from persimmon, which, like hickory, was discovered in America. Demand soon began to exceed supply, however, and successful experiments were made with laminated, composition, and, recently, metal heads. Further protection from the general wear and tear on the clubs came with the use of brass sole plates and insets of bone, ivory and, more economically, plastic.

Hickory was in short supply after the First World War, resulting in experiments with steel, which proved to be a big advance. The steel shaft was legalized in the United States in 1926 and in Britain in 1930. It was much more durable than hickory and mass production quickly brought the arrival of the matched set of clubs with graded shaft-lengths and lofted club-heads, all perfectly balanced.

In the 1930s some players were carrying as many as twenty-five clubs. The Royal and Ancient Golf Club and the United States Golf Association decided that some standard was needed and limited the number to fourteen, which has remained the maximum ever since.

Clothing

The first USGA Women's Amateur golf competition in 1895 was a grand get-together of socially prominent women golfers, dressed in high starched collars and long skirts ballooned by an assortment of petticoats. During this same period the rapidly expanding game was played by male contestants in jackets and ties and everyday, smooth-soled shoes.

In the 1920s, Walter Hagen, an American, changed the styles for both women and men, introducing cardigan sweaters and pullovers in pastel shades and two-tone spiked shoes—altogether a sartorial elegance that set the fashion for the future. The tie was the last relic of the past to depart— Bobby Locke still wore one in his Open championship-winning years of the 1950s.

The International Spread of Golf

Wherever Scots went, they carried their national pastime and the love of their links with them. The game of golf was introduced sporadically over a number of decades to distant outposts of the British Empire and other parts of the world, first by Scotsmen and later by Englishmen.

The international spread of golf largely followed the expansion of the British Empire, which took golf to the four corners of the earth.

The first Golf Club on the European Continent was formed by convalescing Scottish officers in the foothills of the Pyrenees at Pau, France, in 1856. The British took the game to Calcutta as early as 1829 and to Bombay in 1842. The Royal Adelaide Club was begun in Australia in 1871 and Clubs appeared in New Zealand soon thereafter. In 1885 the Royal Cape Club was founded in South Africa by Scottish soldiers and engineers.

Golf arrived in North America through the officers of the Scottish trading ships with the establishment of Royal Montreal, Canada in 1873. By 1876 there were five courses in Canada: at Montreal, Quebec, Toronto, Brantford and Niagara-on-the-Lake.

The British presence in Hong Kong brought the game to the Far East in 1889. It soon spread to Thailand and to Japan, where the first course was established on the lower slopes of Mount Rokko, near Kobe.

While the growth of golf in Asia was initially slow, in recent years this has changed dramatically. Japan has seen spectacular growth in the number of courses, from just seventeen in 1946 to more than 1600 today. Just as Scottish and English golfers initially spread golf all over the world, so Japanese golfers have led the rapid spread of golf courses throughout Asia.

In recent years, the expansion of golf has continued to all parts of the globe — and beyond. In 1971 Captain Alan Shepard, Commander of Apollo 14, hit two shots with a telescopic six iron on the moon. The Royal and Ancient Golf Club of St. Andrews at once sent a telegram reminding him that "before leaving a bunker a player should carefully fill up and smooth over all holes and footprints made by him," failure to do so being a breach of the etiquette of the game!

Golf in the United States

It is clear that golf found its way from Great Britain to North America, but when and by whom it was introduced to the continent is an uncertainty. There were short-lived Golf Clubs in South Carolina and Georgia soon after the American Revolution. Other claims to early courses and Clubs include The Foxburg (Pennsylvania) Country Club, the Dorset (Vermont) Field Club, and other reports from Maryland, Kentucky, Iowa, West Virginia, Florida, New York, Nebraska, and Illinois.

The title of Father of American Golf has generally been given to John Reid, a transplanted Scot, albeit one who had never played golf before coming to this country. However, a friend of Reid's from Scotland, Robert Lockhart, brought over a set of clubs and persuaded Reid to try his hand at the game.

In 1888 Reid and several hardy friends staked out a rough three-hole golf course near his home in Yonkers, New York. Later that year they built a six-hole course in a nearby pasture and formed a golfing organization that they unabashedly named St. Andrew's (with an

Dress fashion for golf in the 1890s reflected everyday clothing styles.

Fred Herd, the U.S. Open champion in 1898.

apostrophe) Golf Club. They did this in the hope that the name would inspire interest in America as effectively as its namesake, St. Andrews, had in Scotland.

The nineteenth hole at St. Andrew's Golf Club in 1892 was an apple tree. The members hung their coats, lunches, and a wicker demijohn containing several pints of Scotland's *other* gift to the world on its branches. The original thirteen members of the club were called the Apple Tree Gang. The Club twice moved before settling at its present site in Mount Hope, New York. Today, St. Andrew's persists in its claim that it is the oldest Golf Club in the United States.

In 1897 St. Andrew's built a new clubhouse, largely financed by Andrew Carnegie. Carnegie loved his new Club and was a rabid golfer. Early on the day he was to sell the Carnegie Steel Corporation to U.S. Steel for $250 million, he played the St. Andrew's course and triumphantly parred its fifth hole for the first time. Later that day, as he pulled up in front of J.P. Morgan's bank, a friend came up, obviously aware of the major business transaction at hand, and said, "I've been hearing great things about you." Carnegie stared in amazement and said, "How did you know I had a par on the fifth today?"

Once golf was introduced to America, its spread was swift and sure. Among the most significant early courses were Shinnecock Hills at Southampton, Long Island, and the Chicago Golf Club. Shinnecock came into being in 1891 after an exhibition inspired three Americans to build a course and incorporate as a Club. The Club offered eighteen holes within a year or so, with a handsome clubhouse designed by the noted architect, Stanford White.

The Chicago Golf Club was one of the first to have eighteen holes. It was begun by Charles Blair Macdonald, one of the most colorful figures in the history of American golf. Macdonald was a founder of the United States Golf Association, first winner of the U.S. Amateur and designer of the great National Golf Links of America.

Shinnecock Hills, The Chicago Golf Club, St. Andrew's, Newport Golf Club in Rhode Island and The Country Club at Brookline, Massachusetts combined to organize the Amateur Golf Association of the United States in 1894, which later became the United States Golf Association (USGA). The following year the first official USGA Championships, both amateur and open were held at the Newport Golf Club for both men and women.

The growth of Golf Clubs in the U.S. spread like wildfire. By 1896 there were over eighty courses in the United States; by 1900 there were 982, with at least one in each of the forty-five states. In fact, by the turn of the century courses in the United States outnumbered those in Britain, although none was comparable in quality to the famous links of Scotland, nor to the heath land courses that would appear in England in the early years of the twentieth century.

John Reid, the Father of American Golf, on the first tee of St. Andrew's Golf Club.

The first photograph of golf in America, taken in November of 1888 near John Reid's home.

The handsome clubhouse at Shinnecock Hills.

During the first decade of the twentieth century, American golf was ruled by foreign-born players. Then, in 1913, came the bombshell that put golf on the front page in America. A twenty-year old amateur and former caddie, Francis Ouimet, defeated the great British professionals Harry Vardon and Ted Ray in a play-off for the U.S. Open Championship. Ouimet became the first amateur to win the Open.

Prior to Ouimet's victory in 1913, there were few, if any, public courses in the United States, and the game was generally regarded as a pastime of the idle rich. But this upset victory by a boy from the wrong side of the tracks changed American attitudes: it created a new respect for the game among the public and helped U.S. golfers rid themselves of an inferiority complex in relation to the British.

In the space of only twenty six years, from 1913 to World War II, golf had gained a strong foothold in the United States and was continuing to grow at a remarkable rate.

The opulent clubhouse at Glen Cove, New York.

Competition

Golf was clearly a competitive game from the very start. Though it was always a pleasure to hit a golf ball about in the company of one's friends, the true delight was in acquiring superior skill and becoming a better player. But how to demonstrate it?

Matchplay was the original score-keeping method, developed during golf's earliest years, prior to the seventeenth century. Each hole was played and the player who hit the ball least often to *hole out* won the hole. The player who won the most holes in a day won the match. A match could be played by two people or four. In the latter case each pair formed a team and hit the ball alternately, playing with one ball against the other team, a form of golf known as a *foursome*.

The first competitions were all single or foursome matches. The competitors were local friends and, one imagines, they played for no stake, or perhaps a very small one. But when the Stuart kings and their courts took up the game in the seventeenth century it became a very fashionable sport, and heavy bets were placed on the outcome of matches. These were usually foursomes, frequently between two noblemen, each playing with a good golfer from a humbler walk of life.

Francis Ouimet at the U.S. Open in 1913.

Though matchplay was the predominant form of golf competition in the sixteenth, seventeenth and eighteenth centuries, *stroke play*, also known as *score play* or *medal play*, (because it was usually played for a medal) was already a part of competition golf by the eighteenth century. In this game, every stroke is counted, from the drive off the first tee to the last putt into the hole on the final green. The winner is the player who completes the course with the least number of strokes. The first stroke play tournament took place at St. Andrews about 1759.

Apart from competing in a few local Scottish tournaments, the only way to make a living as a professional golfer, before the late nineteenth century, was by playing challenge matches. Few amateurs were involved in these competitions because the pros, who were the better players, were best able to attract backers' money. Prize money put up by backers and heavy betting helped the players earn a modest living, along with small retainers from the Clubs for teaching lessons and making clubs. Cold, wet winters spelled lean times for professional competition players.

Real tournament golf, open to all persons with the aim of identifying a champion, started in 1860, when eight professionals competed over three rounds of twelve holes each at Prestwick, in western Scotland. They played for a red morocco leather *challenge belt* that would become the permanent possession of the player who could win the tournament three years running. The idea of competing for a belt probably derived from medieval knights' tournaments, in which the champion's belt symbolized his victory.

This first Open Championship, or British Open, in 1860, was restricted to professionals. But in the following year it became truly open to the world and it has been so ever since. Even in these days of prestigious golfing events, the British Open is regarded by many as *the* championship golf competition in the world.

Competition at St. Andrews in 1849.

Participation in this most daunting of golf competitions was slow to develop. By the time the British Open was fourteen years old, the field of players numbered only thirty. But by 1894 the number of entries had increased to ninety-four. From 1894 until 1914 the British Open was dominated by three outstanding British players: Harry Vardon, John Henry Taylor and James Braid, known as The Great Triumvirate. They became renowned as the greatest golfers of all time.

The role of women in golf's formative years has been documented since 1868 by the North Devon Ladies' Club, established in that year in England. The Club maintained its own nine hole course at Westward Ho! At the time, women's play was limited to alternate Saturdays between the beginning of May and the end of October and to the use of the putter only. Vigorous exercise for women was not approved, and the elaborate fashions of the time made a full swing impracticable.

It was not long before other new women's clubs began to spring up and women were permitted to compete. The London Scottish Ladies, formed in 1872, was eventually responsible for the establishment of a governing authority, the Ladies' Golf Union in 1893. Soon after the Union's formation was announced, an angry gentleman golfer wrote a letter informing its members that, "Constitutionally and physically women are unfitted for golf. The first women's championship will be the last. They are bound to fall out and quarrel on the slightest, or no, provocation." Despite such misguided prognostications, women's golf was a smash success from the start. By 1899 there were 128 ladies' golf clubs in the United Kingdom alone. Women's golf play and competition has flourished ever since, and today matches men's golf in popularity.

Meanwhile, tournament golf was developing in the United States. The U.S. Golf Association was founded in 1894 and the first United States Amateur Championships and U.S. Open Championship (offering a first prize of $150) were held that year. It wasn't until 1911, however, that an American player won the tournament for the first time.

1904 brought an important event for the enhancement of American golfing morale. A U.S. player, Walter J. Travis, unknown in Britain, crossed the Atlantic and won the British Amateur Championship. This was quite an achievement, considering that no American golfers had yet won their own Open, nor, until only two years before, their own Amateur championship.

The ladies of Westward Ho! at Devon, England in the late nineteenth century.

Travis' triumph encouraged other American amateurs to take on the British with the confidence they could beat them. In 1921 an American won the British Open, and the next year the Open was again won by an American, the elegantly dressed Walter Hagen. The eventual U.S. domination of world golf was on its way.

The great size and climate diversity of the United States proved a boon to U.S. professionals. When there was snow in the North the South was warm; when the South became too hot the North was just right for golf. The rounds of tournaments followed the sun and there was competitive action all year round. Because Britain offered only six months of potentially good golf weather, top players often emigrated to the U.S., where there were more events, more money and more months of play. Once born, the U.S. tournament circuit grew by leaps and bounds. Financial rewards for the few at the top became enormous.

After World War II, the yearly golf tournament circuit expanded to include the whole world, as improved air travel made it cheaper, easier and quicker to reach tournaments thousands of miles from home. Many countries, notably Spain and Japan, proved themselves in the process of hosting world tournament golf.

The friendly competitions at St. Andrews of just a few gentlemen pioneers has given way today to a high-powered circuit of major tournaments with world-wide satellite television coverage and prize money in the millions of dollars. Golf as an international sport is here to stay as long as there are fairways to challenge the indomitable spirit of competitors throughout in the world.

Golf's famous triumvirate: J.H. Taylor, James Braid and Harry Vardon.

The Great Players

The first true heroes of the golfing world were England's Great Triumvirate, Harry Vardon, John Henry Taylor and James Braid. These three players dominated the sport for as long as they remained

Elegantly dressed Walter Hagen driving in the 1924 Open at Hoylake.

The greats of two eras — Harry Vardon and Bobby Jones — at Inverness Country Club in Toledo, Ohio for the 1920 U.S. Open.

in the game. All three golfers were associated with Clubs, and spent most of their time giving exhibitions and playing in tournaments.

In 1900 Spalding began to market the Vardon Flyer ball, and brought Vardon and Taylor to the United States for an exhibition tour to promote sales. While on the tour, Vardon won the U.S. Open and Taylor came in second, a circumstance that did nothing to ease the inferiority complex of American professionals. The reputation of the Triumvirate was daunting. They accounted for sixteen British Open titles over twenty-one years, not to mention the twelve times one of the three was running second while another was winning. No one ever again was able to so completely dominate a single championship. Harry Vardon, along with Taylor and Braid, succeeded in raising the quality of golf to a new level, for both players and spectators alike.

The years between the end of World War I and the beginning of the Great Depression were known by various titles including the Roaring Twenties, the Jazz Age and the Era of Wonderful Nonsense. But for sports buffs they were the Golden Age, and for good reason. These were the years of sports heroes such as Babe Ruth, Bill Tilden, Red Grange and Jack Dempsey, who will be remembered as long as games are played, not only for the records they set but also for their dash, style, and colorful presence. Perhaps it was the mood of the times, but these stars possessed an aura that has never been matched. Certainly this was true of golf's great figures of that day—Bobby Jones, Walter Hagen and Gene Sarazen.

The rise in the superiority of American golfers during the roaring twenties, sport's golden decade, was spectacular. The trio of Jones, Hagen and Sarazen accounted for thirty-one major championships between 1914 and 1935, twenty five of them in the nine years from 1922 through 1930. They were America's answer to Britain's triumvirate of Vardon, Taylor and Braid, who won sixteen British Opens in twenty-one years.

One of the reasons for the increasing prestige of U.S. golf was Walter Hagen, undoubtedly the most colorful professional golfer of all time. The Haig, as he was popularly known, won a record number of five PGA titles and a total of eleven major championships. At the same time he won sixty-odd other tournaments and played in more than 1,500 exhibitions. When Hagen won the British Open in 1922, he became the first native-born American to win that famed prize. The Haig won three more British Opens before he retired in the late 1930s.

Hagen was the game's first great box-office attraction. He liked to say he was the first golfer to make a million dollars and spend two million. Prior to Hagen, professionals were scorned and treated badly by many of the game's best amateurs, who considered themselves the better pure players. Because of his refusal to compromise either his game or his career, Hagen led the way in breaking down the social barrier between amateurs and professionals. He was the fashion plate everyone copied. He demanded, and got, large sums for exhibitions and tours, helping considerably to raise the prize money available to professionals.

Above all, Hagen's famous all-night parties just before a crucial match, his chauffeur-driven limousine, his sartorial splendor, his superior gamesmanship and tremendous skill as a player combined to imbue golf with a new dash and color. Hagen brought golf increasingly before the public eye, garnering more newspaper space than golf had enjoyed in all the years before he came on the scene.

In the amateur ranks, the greatest player of all times, Robert Tyre Jones, Jr. blossomed forth in the early twenties. From 1923 to 1930, "Bobby" Jones won thirteen national championships: Four U.S. National Opens, three British Opens, five U.S. National Amateurs, and one British Amateur. Jones was first or second in eight out of nine straight U.S. Opens. The climax of his career came in 1930, when he scored his Grand Slam, the four leading major golf championships of the world—the British and the American Opens and Amateurs—*all in the same year.* This record, as well as his thirteen major championship wins, is unmatched. In 1930, after the Grand Slam, he retired from competitive golf at the age of twenty-eight. Jones received ticker-tape parades and the fan mail of a movie star. He made a series of movie shorts on golf instruction, conceived and helped design the Augusta National course, and inaugurated the Masters tournament.

The last of the Big Three of that glorious era to come on the scene was Gene Sarazen. By the time he was twenty years old he had won both the U.S. Open and PGA Championships. Sarazen was one of only four men to win the four major titles open to professionals. He continued to break par well past his 65th birthday.

By the mid-1930s Americans were looking for successors to Hagen, Jones and Sarazen. In Byron Nelson, Ben Hogan and Sam Snead, the golfing public was again inspired. For the next fifteen years the Scoring Machines, as they were called, dominated U.S. golf, with scores that were almost unbelievable to the veterans from the twenties, even considering the technical advances in equipment.

Women were also very prominent in the early days of the sport. Glenna Collett Vare, who was introduced to golf by her father, had been a swimmer, a diver, and a baseball player on her brother's team. Collett was a promising golfer from the start, but it was 1922 before she won the first of her six U.S. Women's Amateur Championships. In the twenties she was the preeminent American woman player.

The great British champion Joyce Wethered can be viewed as the female counterpart of Bobby Jones. Jones once described her as the finest golfer, man or woman, he had ever seen. Wethered won the English Ladies' Championship five straight times beginning in 1920 and many consider her to be the greatest woman golfer of all time.

Glenna Collett Vare, six time national champion.

Joyce Wethered with the British women's championship trophy she won at Troon in 1925.

The Babe, Mildred Didrikson Zaharias.

Babe Didrikson Zaharias was the first great all-around female professional athlete. Zaharias was the first American woman to capture the British Women's Amateur. At the same time, she also captured the hearts of millions. Besides her golf exploits, she was the star of the 1932 Olympic Games in track and field and excelled at virtually every sport she tried. The Babe was the first woman to hold the post of head professional at a golf club. She helped found the Ladies Professional Golf Association in 1949, and was voted Woman Athlete of the Half Century by the Associated Press in 1949.

Many others were quick to perceive the advantages to be gained from a public association with golf. High on the list were celebrities from the entertainment world. Bing Crosby and Bob Hope were devoted to golf for many years, and Crosby sponsored his own popular tournament as early as 1937. Later, popular entertainers such as Perry Como, Danny Thomas, Andy Williams, Jackie Gleason, Dinah Shore and others began to identify themselves with the game by sponsoring tournaments.

After World War II, golf personalities were more popular than ever. In time, the great golfers of the 1960s and 1970s emerged to reign supreme: Jack Nicklaus and Arnold Palmer from the U.S. and South Africa's Gary Player. Each has contributed greatly to the increasing popularity of the game, which has never looked back since the early days when the very first enthusiasts in Scotland began batting featheries on a primitive links land at St. Andrews. &

The Ladies' Home Journal. *Harrison Fisher. 1909.*

"A work of art cannot be satisfied with being a representation, it should be a presentation."

Jacques Reverdy
French artist, twentieth century

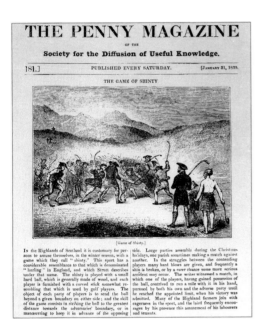

The Penny Magazine. *1835.*

The first magazines were published in France in 1665. Others soon followed around the world, and they were typical of the visually dry and textually dull publications that appeared during the first 200 years of magazine history. Most publishers did not realize the significance of visuals as tools to educate, shape opinions, entertain, and sell greater numbers of their magazines.

During the mid-nineteenth century the magazine began to change from an elitist publication to the main source of popular entertainment for the general public. Instead of speaking primarily to the well-educated upper classes, the magazine addressed a broad cross section of the population. Aided and inspired by the cultural and technical changes of the Industrial Revolution, the new, modern magazine enjoyed a dramatic rise in popularity in Europe, the United States and elsewhere. By 1890 it had begun its most colorful period.

Through the addition of illustrations the periodical achieved a new character and vitality in the Victorian Age. With the emergence of the magazine, art could be disseminated to substantial numbers of people for the first time in history.

Until that time all art forms had been relatively inaccessible to the general public, remaining in the hands of privileged friends and patrons of the artists or publicly displayed in faraway cities. The sport of golf was likewise generally inaccessible up to this time. As the public's appreciation of art grew, the magazine proved to be an important stage for artists of all kinds to depict golf in all its romantic glory.

The magazine cover, like the magazine itself, had been neglected as a decorative element in its early years. But with the increase in vivid dramatic illustrations came the discovery that the magazine cover had important powers to influence and amuse.

Great Britain took the early lead in producing illustrated periodicals during the nineteenth century. Publishers, as well as master engravers and artists, sensed the public's readiness to spend a shilling a copy to enjoy the latest illustrations, which were often eyewitness accounts of current events.

Harper's Weekly. *1912.*

Aubrey Beardsley illustration of ladies' fashion. 1894.

There are two apparent reasons for the emergence of Great Britain as the early leader of illustrated periodicals and books: its efficient communications system for distribution of publications and its educated public to read them. However, other countries soon began to catch up with and eventually surpass Great Britain in the visual arts.

With the emergence of *Frank Leslie's Illustrated Weekly* and *Harper's Weekly*, the modern illustrated periodical was born in America. It took American marketing ingenuity to become the link that propelled the magazine into the hands of vast numbers of people.

The late nineteenth century was a time of great social change during which the traditional class structures were being eroded. Magazines were an important focus for people as they experienced a shifting of social values. Golf was brought to light through accounts and illustrations of early visitors to Scotland and elsewhere.

Perhaps the 1890s should have been called the *more decade.* The nineties brought more money, more leisure, education, sports and entertainment. As travelers discovered golf, it followed that the sport of golf would be extensively offered to the magazine public.

Production of magazines went through revolutionary changes during the late nineteenth century. Until that time, it was a difficult, time-consuming and costly task to produce the visuals accompanying magazine text. Publications would often share the $300 to $500 cost for a full page woodcut with other publishers. This prohibitive cost was reduced as technological changes made economies of scale possible. The same was true with the technological changes in golf equipment, which led to economies of scale and reductions in cost.

A typical magazine illustration took three weeks to complete in the mid-nineteenth century. By 1872 the process of making an illustration from start to finish took one week. Ten years later it had been refined to two days, and by 1900 shortened to a few hours. Photoengraving came into use about this time, radically reducing the time and cost for producing magazine graphics. It reduced a long laborious process to a simple, mechanical one.

In addition to photography, the other important technical advancement for magazine illustrations was the color revolution. Color lithography enabled magazines to display beautiful works of art with a quality never dreamed possible by most people. The color revolution produced intensified public interest in prints, posters and magazine covers. As a result, important artists such as Will Bradley, Edward Penfield, Charles Dana Gibson and Maxfield Parrish were drawn to these media. Other famous illustrators included Harrison Fisher (The Fisher Girl), Howard Chandler Christy (The Christy Girls), Jessie Wilcox Smith (wide-eyed children), and Norman Rockwell (all-American scenes).

Magazines used vivid illustrations to attract readers, showing the Scottish sport of golf in all its picturesqueness, depicting people from all walks of life enjoying the challenge of the sport.

Looking at magazine covers, one can understand the important interaction between the magazine and fine art. Clearly, the magazine, and its cover in particular, comprised an important medium allowing many remarkable artists to test their experimental works in public. The cover also became a medium through which fine art was diffused into a more commercial form, more readily available to the masses.

During the early decades of the twentieth century, the magazine industry flourished. Since radio generally did not enter American households until the early 1920s, magazines enjoyed a captive market. There were fears, of course, that the popularity of radio would completely smother the magazine industry. Fortunately, it did not.

One of the keys to the success of magazine publishing was the increase in advertising, which helped lower the public price of each magazine and, in turn, boosted circulation. Advertisers pumped large sums of money into the industry, as they discovered the buying power of the rising middle class could best be tapped through magazines.

The biggest effect felt by the magazine industry in the 1930s was not that of the Depression or international political tension, but the publication of *Life* magazine in 1936. With 96 pages of photographs and only a minimum of text, *Life* brought photo-journalism into unprecedented importance, as the photographer took the magazine cover away from the illustrator.

This introduction of photographic accounts proved to be decisive. It signaled the beginning of the end of the period of predominance of magazine illustrations. But it was also decisive in bringing forth a new awareness and public enthusiasm for modern golf. ∽

Pictorial Review. *McClelland Barclay. 1932.*

The Illustrated American. *1894.*

Golf match between the Royal Blackheath and London Scottish Clubs at Wimbledon. The Graphic. *1870.*

Golf match on Blackheath. The Illustrated London News. *1870.*

Mr. A.J. Balfour, Captain of the Royal and Ancient Golf Club at St. Andrews. Frank Leslie's Popular Monthly. *1895.*

Collier's Weekly. *Thure de Thulstrup. 1899.*

Harper's. *1898.*

One for the hole — A romance of the fair green. Collier's Weekly. *W.T. Smedley. 1900.*

I've played thirteen! Harper's Weekly. *A.B. Frost. 1898.*

Fore!! Scribner's. *A.B. Frost. 1897.*

Stymie. Scribner's. *A.B. Frost. 1897.*

Dormy Two. Scribner's. *A.B. Frost. 1897.*

A Foursome. Scribner's. *A.B. Frost. 1897.*

In a Bunker. Scribner's. *A.B. Frost. 1897.*

Just Missed It. Scribner's. *A.B. Frost. 1897.*

Ladies' Home Journal. *Thomas Mitchell Peirce. 1901.*

Ladies' Home Journal. *Keller. 1900.*

Harper's Weekly. *A.B. Frost. 1900.*

Winter Golf — "Play the Like in Four!" Harper's Weekly. *A.B. Frost. 1899.*

Harper's Weekly. *1897.*

Has it ever happened to you? Harper's Weekly. *James Montgomery Flagg. 1909.*

Harper's Weekly. *A.B. Frost. 1897.*

Is it customary over here to make any — er — small wager on the results of a match? Munsey's. *Martin Justice. 1911.*

Tournament Day. Harper's Weekly. *A.B. Frost. 1898.*

Puck. *Ehrhart. c. 1902.*

Puck. *Ehrhart. 1902.*

Scribner's. *Harrison Fisher. 1897.*

Scribner's. *Alfred James Dewey. c. 1900.*

John Henry Taylor. Vanity Fair. *1903.*

Hoylake. Vanity Fair. *Spy. 1903.*

Muir. Vanity Fair. *Spy. 1903.*

Horace Hutchinson. Vanity Fair. *Spy. 1903.*

VANITY FAIR Supplement

Mr. R. Maxwell. Vanity Fair. *Spy. 1903.*

James Braid. Vanity Fair. *Spy. 1903.* *Mr. John Ball, Jr.* Vanity Fair. *Lib. 1903.*

Life. *Harold C. Earmshaw. 1914.*

The Canadian. *Bob Dean. 1929.*

Puck. *M. Glackins. 1916.*

Illustrated Sunday Magazine. *F. Earl Christy.* 1910.

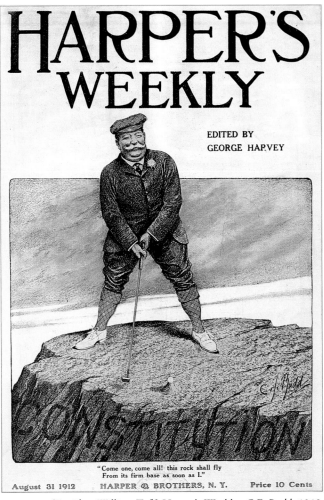

[President William Taft]. Harper's Weekly. *C.F. Budd. 1912.*

The Saturday Evening Post. *Peter Fountain. 1903.*

THE SATURDAY EVENING POST

An Il̶l̶u̶s̶t̶r̶a̶t̶e̶d̶ ̶W̶eekly
Founded A̶.̶D̶.̶ ̶1̶7̶2̶8̶ ̶b̶y̶ ̶B̶aj. Franklin

JULY 17, 1915   **5cts. THE COPY**

In This Number

Mary Roberts Rinehart
Norman Angell, Samuel G. Blythe, Edgar Franklin, Reginald Earle Looker
Leavitt Ashley Knight, Pelham Grenville Wodehouse, Emerson Hough

The Saturday Evening Post. *1915.*

Illustrated Sunday Magazine. *1909.*

COUNTRY GENTLEWOMAN

edited by CAROLINE B. KING

"WHAT DO YOU WANT FOR YOUR GIRL FROM SPORT?" JOHN R. TUNIS, FAMOUS SPORTS WRITER,
TELLS—ON PAGE 21—JUST WHY THIS QUESTION CONCERNS EVERY WOMAN IN THE UNITED STATES

Country Gentlewoman. *Toni Webb. 1935.*

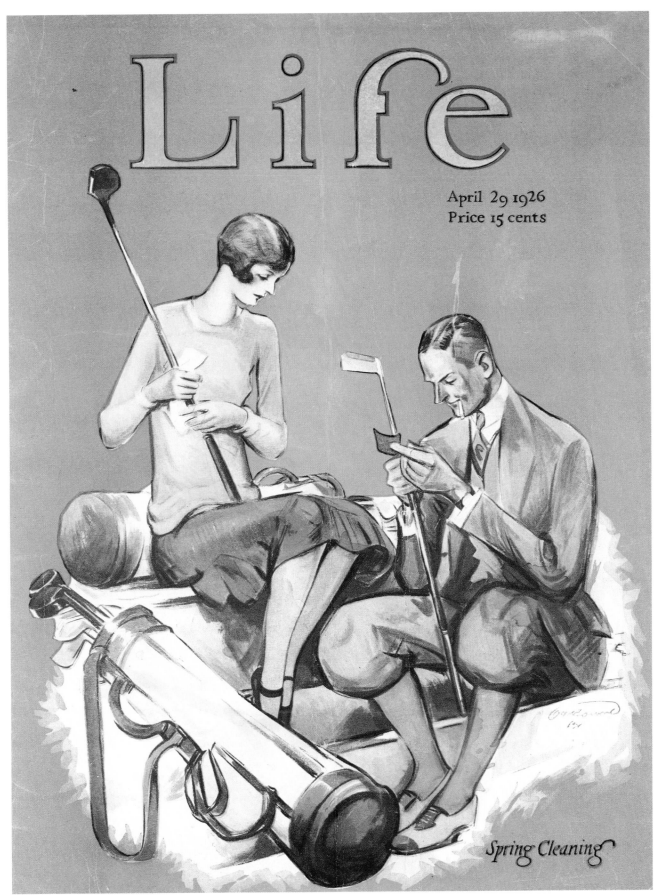

Life. 1926.

Judge. *1921.*

Life. *1927.*

Life. *McCarthy. 1926.*

Inn Dixie. *1935.*

5¢ a copy
September 6, 1930

Collier's
THE NATIONAL WEEKLY

Reply Paid

By Nina
Wilcox
Putnam

The Crack of
Doom

By Don
Marquis

HYMER

Kathleen Norris – Hugh MacNair Kahler – Grantland Rice – Elmer Davis

Collier's. *H. Hymer. 1930.*

"Fore!"

Life. *Coles Phillips. 1920.*

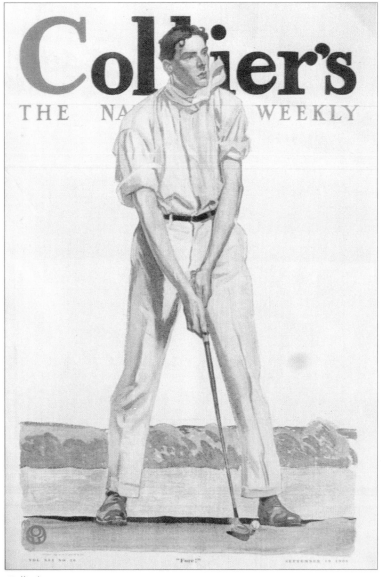

Collier's. *1908.*

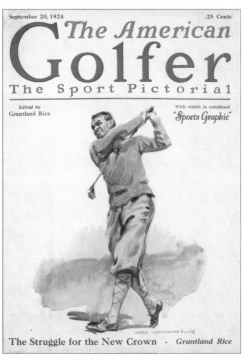

The American Golfer. *James Montgomery Flagg. 1924.*

The DEARBORN INDEPENDENT

Volume 26, Number 25

Five Cents a Copy　　APRIL 10, 1926　　$1.50 a Year

CHRONICLER OF THE NEGLECTED TRUTH

The Dearborn Independent. *Neff. 1926.*

La Vie Parisienne. *Herouard. 1922.*

Life. *Raymond Thayer. 1929.*

Life. *Garrett Price. 1926.*

The Saturday Evening Post. *E.M. Jackson. 1922.*

Woman's Weekly. *J.W. Collins. 1921.*

Collier's. *1931.*

Judge. *1922.*

Judge. *R. John Holmgren. 1924.*

PICTORIAL
REVIEW

AUGUST-1931   TEN CENTS

MARLENE DIETRICH—IN PERSON

An intimate close-up of the internationally popular screen actress

By CORINNE LOWE

Pictorial Review. *McClelland Barclay. 1931.*

OCTOBER, 1931
Volume XLVIII, Number 10

IO Cents By subscription $1.00
In the United States

LADIES' HOME
JOURNAL

By
CLARENCE
BUDINGTON
KELLAND

A New Novel of
Golf and Mystery

OUT OF
BOUNDS

Bradshaw Crandell

Ladies' Home Journal. *Bradshaw Crandell. 1931.*

The Canadian Magazine. *John Clymer. 1933.*

Judge. *Ed Graham. 1931.*

Judge. *Ed Graham. 1931.*

Life. *Gilbert Bunch. 1931.*

Life. *Dorothy McKay. 1934.*

Life. *1933.*

Capper's Farmer. *John F. Kernan. 1938.*

Golfing. *Lichty. 1933.*

The New Yorker. *Constantin Alajálov. 1939.*

Liberty. *1939.*

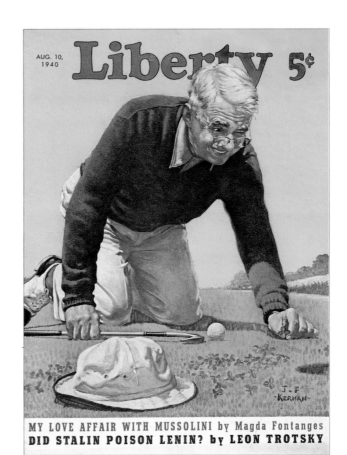

Liberty. *John F. Kernan. 1940.*

SEPT. 28, 1940

Liberty 5¢

HOW JAPAN PLANS TO CONQUER AMERICA by Carl Crow

MURDER ON THE DIAMOND by Joe Medwick

Liberty. *David Berger. 1940.*

Bovril. c. 1900.

*"Advertising is now so near to perfection
that it is not easy to propose any improvement."*

Samuel Johnson, 1759

Abraham and Straus. 1901.

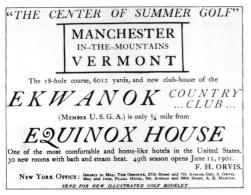

Equinox House. 1901.

*I*n spite of Dr. Johnson's prophesy more than two centuries ago, advertising has indeed seen vast changes and improvements. It has evolved into a major cultural part of our society today, with U.S. advertisers alone spending well over $50 billion a year to promote and sell their goods and services.

Advertising, destined to be the omnipresent, most characteristic and most remunerative form of American literature, did not come into its own until the second half of the nineteenth century.

Prior to the U.S. Civil War, with the factory system still in its infancy, agriculture was the dominant source of national wealth. The market for the products of these early manufacturing and agricultural enterprises was generally the people living in the village, town or city immediately surrounding the producing center.

A fledgling distribution network existed to carry these products to other markets (there were more than 30,000 rail miles in the U.S. in 1860), but there was little demand for its use other than for agricultural products. At this early stage in American manufacturing, sophisticated distribution of goods was not yet developed.

In a selling environment, in which producers were assured of a larger market than their production capacities could meet, it is not surprising to find that most manufacturers did not attempt to differentiate their own products from similar goods. Their products usually carried no identifying brands or marks, and were normally sold by local retailers from bulk lots, along with the products of other producers.

With the majority of producers thus enjoying an assured market, the small amount of advertising undertaken during this pre-war period was placed by retailers attempting to reach customers in their stores' immediate geographic areas. The medium for carrying these factual-only notices was the local newspaper. Aside from printed notices and posters, this was the only practical choice available.

The U.S. Civil War accelerated a trend towards industrialization, and for the first time there was some tentative use of advertising beyond the retail level. With the completion of the transcontinental railroad, the age of advertising had truly begun.

At the outset of the 1880s manufacturers were blessed by blossoming sales. They had just emerged from a decade that had seen the invention of the telephone, the incandescent lamp and significant innovations in factory products. In 1880 alone there were applications for more than 13,000 copyrights and patents, giving rise to an ever-increasing stream of new products from mills and factories.

The potential consumer markets for these goods were also increasing at a dramatic rate, expanding with the transportation capabilities provided by thousands of miles of railroads and roads throughout the ever-enlarging American nation.

In order to achieve effective distribution of their products, manufacturers needed an advertising medium that could reach all sections of their expanded market area. Such a medium was the national magazine, transported by the railroad lines into the American towns, where store shelves carried branded products brought by the same rails.

The increasingly popular tool of advertising in magazines led to some spectacular sales successes by its regular users. This success led to a further increase in advertising, which in turn helped lower the public price of each magazine and, as a result, boosted circulation. Advertisers pumped large sums of money into the industry, as they discovered that the buying power of the rising middle class could best be tapped through magazines. Thus, advertising was inextricably tied to the growth of newspapers, magazines and increased consumerism.

Advertising also changed the entire concept of magazine publishing. Up to this time publishers had generally relied on the readers themselves to pay for the cost of the magazines through the newsstand and subscription prices. But as advertising revenues continued to reward the confidence of advertisers in the medium's ability to deliver a selling message, this concept changed. Thus, in 1890 a publisher was quoted as saying, "If I can get a circulation of 400,000, I can afford to give my magazine away to anyone who'll pay the postage." The publisher was no longer simply creating a medium of entertainment, but rather a profitable advertising vehicle that would reach a certain number of potential customers and fully fund his magazine.

Pond's Extract. c. 1900.

As advanced technology permitted low-cost reproduction of illustrations and color lithography, advertisers became increasingly competitive in their creativity. This led to new found uses of graphics in advertising, in order to give the reader a visual image of the product or to evoke a positive-feeling towards the product.

It is not difficult to understand why the English Prime Minister, William Gladstone, insisted on sending to America for magazines, even when English editions were available. It was the American advertisements that fascinated him.

During this period, golf was associated with a life of leisure, manners and good taste. Advertisers of many products incorporated these lifestyle images into their product messages through the use of golf illustrations. The visual associations consumers made when seeing golf graphics created increased interest in the sport itself. As the public was hungrily trying new consumer products, they were equally enthusiastic to learn of the exciting and challenging new sport from Scotland.

During the 1920s and 1930s advertising art came into its own as never before in history. Greater freedom and larger budgets allowed outstanding artists to use golf to enrich the appeal of all useful objects. Manufacturers hired some of the best illustrators and artists to create the visual messages they desired.

The illustrations that follow in this volume are wonderful examples of the graphic advances used in advertising during golf's popular growth years. They invite us to enter a world where one can ward off the ailments of old age on the golf course by using Pabst Extract—"the best tonic," take a luxury cruise to golf in Bermuda for as little as $60, drive the latest model Franklin Sedan or Ford Coupe to the club, or feel that it is "as good as a hole in one" to have a tube of Ben-Gay handy at the nineteenth. At the same time they allow us to appreciate how colorful and evocative such a world might be. ∽

A.G. Spalding & Bros. c. 1900.

John Hancock Life Insurance Company. 1901.

The Equitable Life Assurance Society. Maud Stamm. 1902.

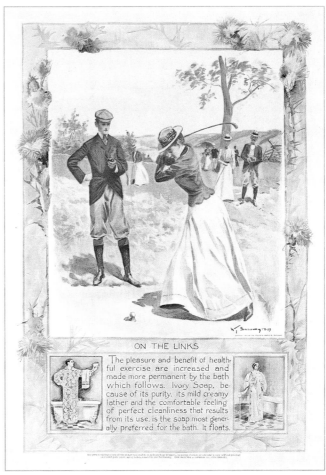

Procter and Gamble Company. 1900.

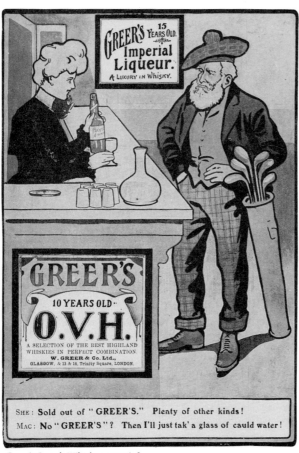

Greer's Scotch Whiskey. 1904.

Cadbury Limited. Cecil Aldin. 1900.

American Tobacco Company. 1900.

Pabst Brewing Company. 1909.

The Coca-Cola Company. 1905.

The Coca-Cola Company. 1906.

Pinehurst Resort. 1903.

Lackawanna Railroad. 1905.

American Tobacco Company. 1913.

Great Eastern Railway. John Hassall. c. 1920.

J.C. Eno, Ltd. 1918.

Depollier Watch Company. J.O. Todahl. 1923.

An admired grace of line and contour

SEEING the new Ford as it speeds along the broad highway or parked proudly beside the cool green of the Country Club, you are impressed by its flowing grace of line and contour. There is about it, in appearance and perform-ance, a substantial excellence which sets it apart and gives it character and position unusual in a low-priced car. To women especially, its safety, its comfort, its reliability and its surprising ease of operation and control have put a new joy in motoring.   «   «   «   «   «   «   «   «

THE NEW FORD COUPE

The Ford Motor Company. 1930.

Studebaker Corporation of America. Harry Slater. 1925.

Franklin Automobile Company. 1920.

The Coca-Cola Company. 1917.

Paris Medicine Company. 1928.

Thomas Leeming & Company. 1926.

Liggett & Myers Tobacco Company. 1914.

Meredith Publishing Company. 1934.

North British Rubber Company. 1932.

Golf de Sarlabot. Rene Vincent. c. 1935.

Montana-Vermala. c. 1930.

Italy. Max Minow. 1931.

B. Altman & Company. 1929.

Abercrombie & Fitch Company. 1927.

Gossard
Corsets and Brassieres

The Gossard Line of Beauty

No matter how loosely draped her raiment, how much fashion conceals the figure, correct carriage, proper poise, and comfort itself, demand proper corseting—Gossard corseting.

No matter what the occasion or the costume, whether gowned for social function, or an afternoon at golf, she must retain the natural line of womanhood's identity—the Gossard line—that rounds from armpit in at the waist, and then sweeps over hip downward.

No matter what her age, or the style of the moment, if a woman would be graceful, she *must* have that youth-line which Gossards give and preserve.

No matter where she lives, the modern woman will find a good store that features Gossards—an expert corsetiere, who knows at a glance how she should be fitted, what Gossard model she should wear, that the Gossard Line of Beauty, the youthful figure line, may be preserved.

The H. W. Gossard Co., Chicago, New York, San Francisco, Toronto, London, Sydney, Buenos Aires
Copyright, 1924

H.W. Gossard Company. 1924.

KUPPENHEIMER FAMOUS FIFTY SUITS

These suits at $50 prove the Kuppenheimer skill. You feel the *extra value* in the fabrics, feel it in the comfortable modeling. You see it in the fresh new styles, in the all-silk stitching, in the unusual respect for detail. Young men will find the new colors - the new lines - and a new standard of value in the Famous Fifties.

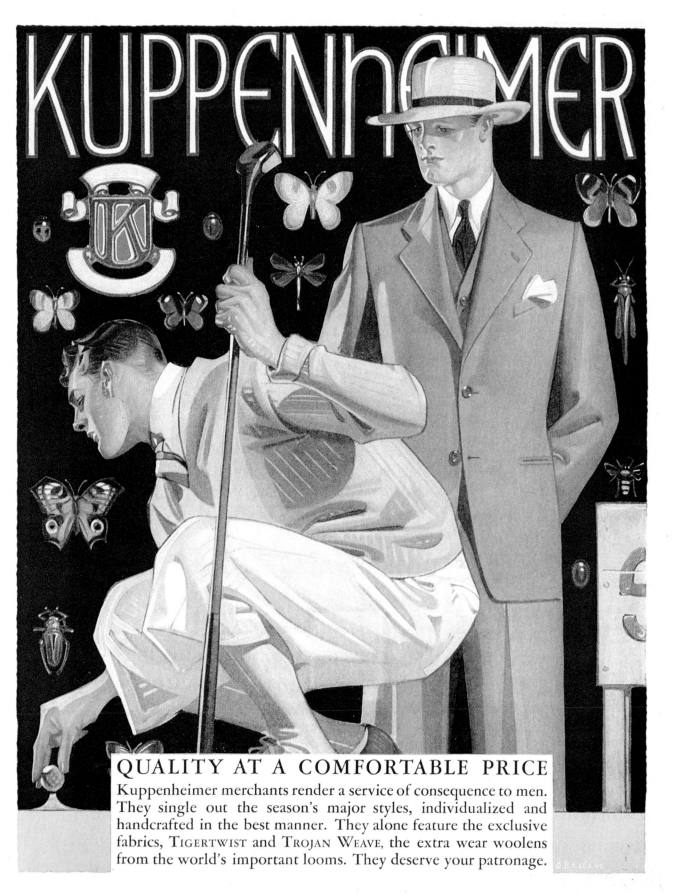

QUALITY AT A COMFORTABLE PRICE

Kuppenheimer merchants render a service of consequence to men. They single out the season's major styles, individualized and handcrafted in the best manner. They alone feature the exclusive fabrics, TIGERTWIST and TROJAN WEAVE, the extra wear woolens from the world's important looms. They deserve your patronage.

Kuppenheimer. 1928.

*M*URRAY has elevated motor car bodycraft to a fine art—at the same time achieving third place in large scale production.

The Murray Corporation of America ~ Detroit

Coach Work by Murray

The Murray Corporation of America. 1927.

Liggett & Myers Tobacco Company. Tepper. 1928.

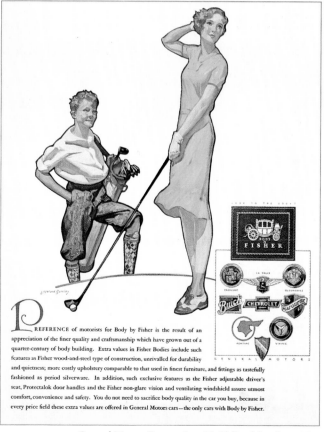

General Motors Corporation. McClelland Barclay. 1930.

Cypress Point Course, 18th Green, looking south of Clubhouse

Winter at Del Monte, Home of Eternal Springtime

"One sobs of Sorrento and Taormina...or the French Riviera and they are as nothing when one sees the cliffs...the mountains...and the cypresses of the Monterey coastline."*

Here, in your own social environment, you may indulge your every fancy in outdoor sports. At your disposal are polo fields, tennis courts, swimming pools, dazzling white beaches, bridle paths through the tall trees, unmatched motor roads, and the world-famed 17-Mile Drive.

Here, too, are four renowned golf courses, including the newly remodeled Pebble Beach Championship Course, where will be played the 1929 National Amateur Championship. Golf is played 365 days a year at Del Monte.

HOTEL DEL MONTE

(Del Monte Lodge, Pebble Beach)

Monterey Peninsula, California

S. F. B. Morse, President   Carl S. Stanley, Manager

DEL MONTE PROPERTIES COMPANY

Hotel Del Monte, Del Monte   Crocker Building, San Francisco

Adjoining Monterey, ancient Spanish capital, on the historic Monterey Peninsula 125 miles south of San Francisco, 350 miles north of Los Angeles

*Quoted from Addison Mizner, nationally-known architect of Florida, who resides during a portion of the year at his Pebble Beach home.

Hotel Del Monte. 1928.

October

In these days of defined standards and precision manufacture, it is pleasant to contemplate the golf ball. This useful article in the days of its youth was constructed of leather and 'stuffed with as many featheris as will fill a hat'. Whose hat—and whose feathers—was not stated and the ruling, in consequence, would seem to leave a certain scope for individuality. But the game was becoming organised. The middle of the 18th century saw the beginnings of that great institution, the Golf Club, of which there are now in Great Britain upwards of 2,000. Two thousand Golf Clubs—and two thousand Honorary Secretaries chasing *x* thousand subscriptions! You can save yours the trouble by using the Midland Bank Standing Orders service, which will pay all such items for you automatically on their due dates.

MIDLAND BANK LIMITED

2,170 branches in England and Wales

HEAD OFFICE: POULTRY, LONDON, E.C.2

Midland Bank Limited. [golfer from mid 18th c.] 1958.

This Complete Change of Scene gives you a REAL VACATION.

THIS summer get away from all the accustomed sights and scenes and people! Above all get away from heat waves, bill-boards, crowded beaches and boardwalks, filling stations, and traffic jams. Bermuda has none of these! It's the grand-est spot in summer, for here are over 150 coral isles in mid-ocean, where you find no extreme heat, no rainy spells, no hay fever, no automobiling, no factories, no subways. Give your mind the tonic of a new environment, your eyes the blessing of in-describably lovely scenery, and your nerves the benefit of restfulness and relaxation. The Bermuda trip costs as little as $60 round-trip on luxury liners, and all hotel rates are at their lowest now. Your American dollars buy full value here. *Compare costs, and you will decide on Bermuda!* • •

For beautiful Bermuda booklet in colours, free and postpaid, consult any travel agency, or Furness Ber-muda Line, Munson Steamship Line, Canadian National Steamships, or The Bermuda Trade Devel-opment Board, 230 Park Avenue, New York. In Canada, 105 Bond Street, Toronto. • • •

BERMUDA

Bermuda Tourist Agency. 1940.

Le Touquet. c. 1930.

Designed by Walter Hagen, the world's premier golfer—bench made in limited quantities by artisans these de luxe matched and registered woods and irons are authentic copies of the clubs used by Walter Hagen in all matches.

THE L. A. YOUNG COMPANY ◆ ◆ DETROIT
Makers of Walter Hagen Golf Equipment

L.A. Young Company. 1929.

L.A. Young Company. 1929.

USA. 1910.

HISTORY OF THE PICTURE POSTCARD

"When archaeologists of the thirtieth century begin to excavate...ruins..., they will focus their attention on the picture postcard as the best means of penetrating the spirit of the...era. They will collect and collate thousands of these cards and they will reconstruct our epoque from the strange hieroglyphics and images they reveal, spared by the passage of time."

James Douglas
English journalist, 1907

Typical greeting card. c. 1910.

$\mathcal{P}$icture postcards originated in Europe in the early 1870s. Production increased in the 1890s with the introduction of new printing techniques and the extension of licenses to private industry to publish postcards. Collotype printing became available on an industrial scale, which led to a proliferation of photographic postcards and color lithography.

Social and cultural factors encouraged the growth of postcards well into the twentieth century. The brevity of the verbal message and the presence of the illustration to augment the written word, by amplifying its meaning or charging it with allusions, were among the reasons for the extraordinary popularity of postcards.

The appearance of the postcard brought about some interesting changes in Victorian and Edwardian letter-writing habits. A letter's contents were concealed inside an envelope, which was considered an improper means of communication for young lovers. A postcard, on the other hand, made it possible to inspect what was written and was therefore more acceptable.

"Like many great inventions," observed the English journalist James Douglas in 1907, "the postcard has brought a silent revolution in our habits. It has freed us unexpectedly from the fatigue of writing letters. There is no space for courtesy."

The postcard became a means of picturesque documentation at a low price, and it was coveted by millions of collectors worldwide. Postcards served as a substitute for those who could not afford first-hand experiences of the places and the subjects represented in them. At the turn of the century, postcard stalls or kiosks were a common sight in public gardens and exhibition parks in European cities, as were postcard salesmen passing along trains, or from table to table in cafes and restaurants.

Woman golfer. 1908.

Before 1907 writing was generally not permitted on the address and stamp side of the postcard (the reverse side of the graphic). Senders of cards had to write their message over the image on the front (graphic) side. In 1907 it became permissible for the writer to use the newly created divided back side for the message, keeping the graphic image clean for the recipient and for posterity.

The golden age of the picture postcard ran from 1898 to the end of the First World War in 1918. During those twenty years many artists and photographers in Europe, the United States and elsewhere developed graphics for postcard publishers. The postcard made both art and photography accessible to the general public.

Women assumed a central role in postcard iconography, and they were popularized by postcard artists in many different situations. Artists often escaped into fantasy with their symbolic and sublime elevations of women into stylized, idealized beings. Significantly, the woman was the principal subject in most illustrators' work, even when there was a man at her side.

Children also figured prominently in postcards throughout the world. In most cases, the image of childhood, with its uninhibited joy in living, its implicit message of hope for the future, and its innocence and openness, was bound up with such messages or greetings as: "Happy Christmas," "Happy Easter" and "Happy New Year."

Sport in general, including golf, has always been a major theme of picture postcards. Participatory sport emerged as a new phenomenon around the turn of the century, its mass appeal becoming synonymous with modernism. Sport was a heroic activity, and golf became an intensely popular postcard subject worldwide.

The postcard was also a means of promoting or reflecting trends in current fashion. As such, postcards are valuable records of golf fashions for both men and women throughout the historic period covered in this volume.

With the availability of photographic postcards, golf course photos became a popular subject for many postcard publishers, bring the view closer to the beauty on the course. Many golf resorts, recognizing the benefits of worldwide attention and publicity, published their own golf picture postcards to promote their tourist facilities and to further the glamorous appeal of the sport.

Postcards became important documents for revealing the international spread of golf as a popular sport. Without the availability of this medium, much of the populace would have had no resource for discovering the excitement of golf.

While collections of postcards in public museums exist today, the collection of cards is primarily the domain of individuals who buy and trade cards, much as their grandparents did generations ago. Now many collectors also do so to preserve the history of times past.

When viewed closely, each postcard in this collection has a story to tell. The scenery, characters and action scenes are static, but they can be brought to life vividly with a bit of imagination and with close attention to the depictions of clothing styles, golf equipment and locations. Through close observation these images can greatly enhance our ability to imagine the experience of golf as it existed around the turn of the century. ✍

Europe. 1912.

A GOLF CHAMPION

England. C.W. Barber. 1913.

USA. F. Earl Christy. c. 1910.

USA. F. Earl Christy. c. 1910.

France. X. Sager. c. 1910.

USA. 1908.

England. c. 1910.

England. c. 1910.

USA. 1909.

USA. 1907.

USA. 1907.

Europe. c. 1910.

Europe. c. 1910.

USA. F. Earl Christy. 1905.

USA. F. Earl Christy. 1908.

England. Archie Gunn. 1906.

England. Archie Gunn. 1906.

England. c. 1910.

A NICE PARTNER FOR A LONG ROUND.

England. 1912.

USA. 1910.

USA. 1912.

England. Archie Gunn. c. 1906.

USA. 1910.

USA. 1907.

USA. c. 1910.

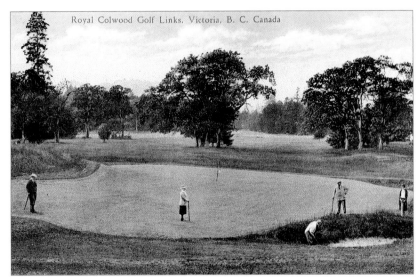

Canada. c. 1910.

USA. 1905.

England. c. 1910.

USA. 1904.

USA. c. 1900.

USA. 1900.

USA. 1900.

USA. 1897.

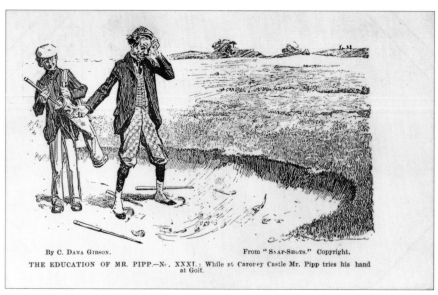

USA. C. Dana Gibson. c. 1900.

England. c. 1910.

USA. 1910.

England. c. 1910.

USA. c. 1910.

Zaïre. c. 1910.

USA. 1910.

USA. c. 1915.

England. c. 1915.

USA. F. Earl Christy. c. 1910.

USA. 1912.

England. c. 1905.

England. c. 1905.

Belgium. c. 1935.

The Netherlands. c. 1910.

THE GOLF PLAYER
This young man has " golfitis " bad,
His case it is really quite sad;
  He calls the small laddie
  Who attends him his " caddie."
And he simply lives for this fad!

USA. 1906.

"I'd even give up a round of Golf for you!"

USA. c. 1910.

USA. c. 1910.

USA. c. 1910.

USA. c. 1910.

QUI OSERAIT SE MESURER A MOI?
WIE DURFT ME UITDAGEN?
WHO DARES TO CHALLENGE ME?

Belgium. c. 1910.

IT'S EASY ENOUGH
TO BE PLEASANT
WHEN YOU'RE STICKING
TO 3'S AND 4'S,
BUT THE MAN WORTH WHILE
IS THE MAN WHO CAN SMILE,
AND STICK DOWN
HIS ACTUAL SCORE.

*Que votre inexpérience
n'altère pas votre bonne humeur!*

England. Mabel Lucie Attwell. c. 1915.

France. 1910.

USA. c. 1910.

USA. 1909.

Cuba. c. 1910.

Scotland. 1905.

USA. c. 1910.

England. c. 1905.

England. c. 1905.

England. c. 1905.

England. c. 1905.

England. c. 1905.

England. c. 1905.

USA. c. 1935.

France. c. 1920.

ACKNOWLEDGEMENTS

Most of the artwork and graphic materials reproduced in this book are from the personal collection of the author. Ownership of and permission to use these and other materials reproduced herein are acknowledged below. While the publisher makes every effort possible to publish full and correct information for every work, in some cases errors may occur. The publisher regrets any such errors but must disclaim any liability in this regard.

The American Tobacco Company.

Cadbury. Courtesy of Cadbury Limited. Cadbury's is a registered trademark of Cadbury Limited.

Chesterfield. Liggett Group Incorporated.

Coca-Cola. Coca-Cola is a registered trademark of The Coca-Cola Company and is used with permission.

Equitable Life Assurance. The Equitable Life Assurance Society of the United States Archives.

Fatima. Liggett Group Incorporated.

General Motors. Reprinted with permission of General Motors Corporation.

Hotel Del Monte. Reproduction courtesy of Pebble Beach Company.

H.W. Gossard Company.

Ladies' Home Journal. © 1931, Meridith Corporation. All rights reserved. Reprinted from Ladies' Home Journal magazine.

Ivory Soap. Courtesy of Procter & Gamble. Reproduced with permission.

Midland Bank. Reproduced by kind permission of Midland Bank PLC.

Pabst Brewing Company.

Studebaker. Cooper Industries.

Walter Hagen Golf Clubs. © Wilson Sporting Goods Company.

INDEX